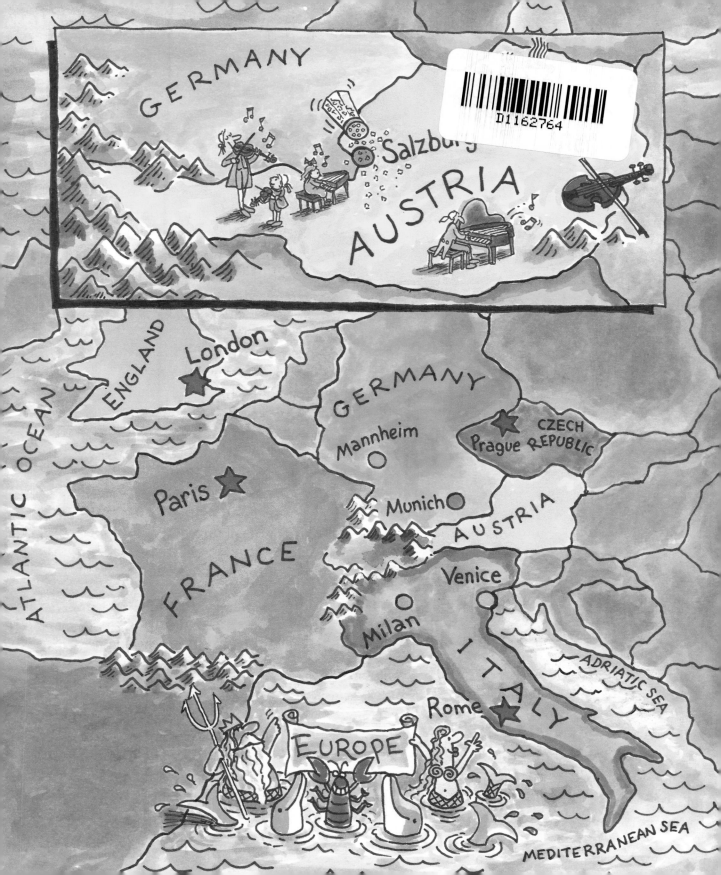

TIMELINE OF WOLFGANG AMADEUS MOZART'S LIFE

1756 Wolfgang Amadeus Mozart is born in Salzburg, Austria.

1759 At age three, Wolfgang begins to play the clavier.

1761 Wolfgang composes his first music pieces and performs in front of a small audience.

1762 Wolfgang learns to play the violin before his father has a chance to teach him! Mr. Mozart takes his children to Vienna where they play for the Empress Maria Theresa. They spend the next few years performing throughout Europe.

1764 Wolfgang composes his first symphony.

1768 Wolfgang composes his first opera.

1773 The prince-archbishop of Salzburg hires Wolfgang to be his concertmaster. Mozart composes new music, conducts the orchestra, and plays violin.

THIS WAY

1777 Wolfgang leaves his job. He goes with his mother to other music centers in Europe, hoping to get more attention and find a better job.

1778 Wolfgang's mother dies while they are visiting Paris.

1781 Wolfgang quits his job and moves to Vienna. He falls in love with Constanze Weber.

1782 Wolfgang and Constanze get married. Over the next five years, Wolfgang composes piano concertos, symphonies, string quartets, and a successful opera.

1788 -1790 Mozart is now famous all over Europe. Even so, he never seems to have enough money. He works hard composing symphonies and operas.

1791 Wolfgang composes *The Magic Flute* and begins his *Requiem*. He is ill and totally overworked. Sadly, he dies in Vienna at the age of thirty-five.

UP HERE

GETTING TO KNOW
THE WORLD'S
GREATEST COMPOSERS

WOLFGANG AMADEUS

MOZART

WRITTEN AND ILLUSTRATED BY MIKE VENEZIA

CONSULTANT
DONALD FREUND, PROFESSOR OF COMPOSITION,
INDIANA UNIVERSITY SCHOOL OF MUSIC

CHILDREN'S PRESS®

An Imprint of Scholastic Inc.

For Sam Venezia

Picture Acknowledgements
Music on the cover, Stock Montage, Inc.; 3, Joseph Lange, oil on canvas, 1789, © Internationale Stiftung Mozarteum, Salzburg; 7, Michel-Barthelemy Ollivier, *In the Salon of 4 Mirrors at the Temple*, 1764, Louvre; 8, North Wind Picture Archives; 9, Bettmann Archives; 13 (both paintings), Pietro Antonio Lorenzoni, oil on canvas, 1763, © Internationale Stiftung Mozarteum, Salzburg; 16, J. Dublessis, Louvre; 19, Bettmann Archive; 21, Anonymous, oil on canvas, © Internationale Stiftung Mozarteum, Salzburg; 24, Bettmann Archive; 25, North Wind Picture Archives; 26, Hans Hansen, oil on canvas, 1802, © Internationale Stiftung Mozarteum, Salzburg; 27, 29, AKG London; 30, Bettmann Archive; 31, San Francisco Opera, Mozart's *Don Giovanni*, 1991, photo by Mary Sohl; 32, Bettmann Archive

Library of Congress Cataloging-in-Publication Data

Names: Venezia, Mike, author, illustrator.
Title: Wolfgang Amadeus Mozart / written and illustrated by Mike Venezia.
Description: Revised edition. | New York : Children's Press, 2017. | Series:
  Getting to know the world's greatest composers | Includes index.
Identifiers: LCCN 2016045671| ISBN 9780531220580 (library binding) | ISBN
  9780531222409 (pbk.)
Subjects: LCSH: Mozart, Wolfgang Amadeus, 1756-1791—Juvenile literature. |
  Composers—Austria—Biography—Juvenile literature.
Classification: LCC ML3930.M9 V46 2017 | DDC 780.92 [B] —dc23 LC record available at
  https://lccn.loc.gov/2016045671

All rights reserved. Published in 2017 by Children's Press, an imprint of Scholastic Inc.
Printed in The United States of America 113

1 2 3 4 5 6 7 8 9 10 R 26 25 24 23 22 21 20 19 18 17

A portrait of Wolfgang Amadeus Mozart
at about age thirty-three

Wolfgang Amadeus Mozart was born in Salzburg, Austria, in 1756. Many people think he was the greatest composer who ever lived. Even though Mozart's music was very popular during his time, he often had to struggle to make a living.

The type of music that Wolfgang Amadeus Mozart played and composed is known as classical music. It was usually written for an occasion like an emperor's court dance or a princess's wedding, or a special church occasion, or an opera. Royal families and other wealthy people who hired composers and musicians were known as patrons.

Many of these wealthy people loved being entertained by music so much that they even had their own orchestras! Unfortunately, most patrons thought of musicians as servants, no matter how talented they were, and paid them very little money.

Classical music in the 1700s had to follow certain rules to be acceptable in the palaces and royal courts of Europe. Even though people loved to be entertained by music, they didn't like many surprises. They expected to hear familiar forms of music, like symphonies, concertos, or sonatas. For royal dances, the music had to be light and happy. For background music at a gathering, it had to be clear and simple, and not too loud. No one wanted it to get in the way of their conversations. Because of these rules, some classical music sounded controlled and not very interesting.

Wolfgang, age ten, performing for French royalty in Paris in 1766

Great composers like Mozart, however, were able to follow the rules of classical music and still create musical masterpieces. They experimented and found ways to put their personal feelings of love, sadness, or fun into classical music and make it very exciting and beautiful.

Wolfgang Amadeus Mozart had quite a remarkable childhood. He and his sister, Nannerl, who was four years older, traveled all over with their parents, playing music for the royal families of Europe. Wolfgang's father, Leopold Mozart, was a composer and violinist in the court of the prince-archbishop of Salzburg.

Mr. Mozart was happily surprised to find that his daughter had a special talent when he began giving her clavier lessons. A clavier is a keyboard instrument similar to a piano. Nannerl quickly learned to play the most difficult pieces.

Wolfgang and his sister Nannerl

Mr. Mozart was *really* surprised, though, when he noticed Wolfgang trying to play the same pieces Nannerl had been practicing. When he was only three years old, Wolfgang Amadeus Mozart already had an unusual understanding of music. By the time he was six, he had learned to play the violin perfectly!

Also at age six, Wolfgang wrote a concerto, a difficult musical form even for an experienced grown-up to write. Mr. and Mrs. Mozart soon realized Wolfgang and Nannerl were different from other children.

In 1762, when Wolfgang was six and Nannerl was ten, Mr. Mozart decided it was time to travel and show his talented children to the world.

$\mathbf{T}$rips during this time were
very difficult—and even
dangerous. Sometimes coaches
could travel only a few miles a
day because of breakdowns or
bumpy, rut-filled roads.

It was cold much of the time, and the inns where the Mozarts stayed at night were uncomfortable. Fortunately, Wolfgang and Nannerl loved performing for audiences so much that they never seemed to mind.

Wolfgang at age six

Nannerl at age eleven

They also enjoyed seeing the great cities of Europe, like Vienna, Paris, London, Brussels, and Munich.

Some people thought Mr. Mozart was taking advantage of his children by making them work hard for money. But Leopold Mozart was a good father who really loved his children and was concerned about their future. He felt that if Wolfgang and Nannerl became famous at an early age, they would have a better chance of making livings as musicians when they grew up.

Making enough money was always a problem for the Mozarts.

Even when audiences went wild over their performances, the Mozart children were often paid with gifts. What Mr. Mozart really needed was money to pay for travel, hotels, clothing, and food.

During his many journeys, Wolfgang wrote lots of new pieces and learned about the music of other countries. In London, England, he studied the music of the great composer George Frideric Handel. In Germany, he learned about mixing different tunes into the same piece of music.

This is called counterpoint. Everything was going well, but then something happened. In 1768, Wolfgang was asked to compose and conduct an opera in Vienna for the Emperor Joseph II.

A portrait that suggests Mozart at about age twelve

For some reason, the emperor's musicians started to give Wolfgang a hard time. They may have been jealous, or afraid they would look bad being directed by a twelve-year-old boy. They caused so many annoying problems that Mr. Mozart gave up trying to put the opera together and took Wolfgang home to Salzburg.

Another problem was that Wolfgang and Nannerl were growing up. People didn't find them quite as cute and remarkable as they once had. Wolfgang knew he would have to amaze people now by writing and playing the best music ever—which is just what he did.

In 1769, Mr. Mozart thought it would be a good idea to take one more trip. This time, just he and Wolfgang would go to Italy.

Nannerl, Wolfgang, and Leopold Mozart

It was decided that Nannerl would stay home with her mother.

Italy was the most important music center of Europe. In Rome, Florence, Naples, and Venice, Wolfgang saw the great Italian operas and heard the clear, delicate melodies of the Italian musical style. Mr. Mozart thought he might be able to get Wolfgang a position in an important Italian court, but it never worked out.

Mr. Mozart really involved himself in Wolfgang's life, and spent lots of time trying to get the best job he could for his son. Leopold Mozart meant well, but didn't give Wolfgang much of a chance to do anything on his own. When they returned home from Italy, Wolfgang was able to get a job with his father in the archbishop's court orchestra. Things were OK until a new archbishop took over.

Archbishop Colloredo

Archbishop Heironymous Colloredo never appreciated Wolfgang Mozart's wonderful talent. He was often rude to Wolfgang, and ordered him to write all kinds of boring musical pieces, sometimes at the last minute.

Wolfgang was very unhappy during this time. Much to his father's disappointment, he wanted to quit his job and travel to kingdoms and cities where he had been a big hit as a child.

Wolfgang really wanted to have the freedom to find his own jobs and make his own decisions about what kind of music he would write and play. Mr. Mozart finally agreed that Wolfgang could go on the trip if his mother went along too. Mr. Mozart wanted his wife to keep an eye on their son, to make sure he didn't waste all his money.

Wolfgang Amadeus Mozart was able to compose and perform some of the greatest music ever, but when it came to handling money, he didn't do very well. Wolfgang loved to spend money by giving parties, going on dates, and buying expensive clothing and wigs. He also loved playing games of all kinds, such as billiards and lawn bowling.

Anna Maria Mozart, Wolfgang's mother

In some of the cities that Wolfgang visited, he continued to amaze audiences. But in other cities, no one seemed to care that much about his music anymore. Wolfgang was becoming upset. In Paris, the worst thing of all happened. Mrs. Mozart became ill, and after a short time, died. Wolfgang was deeply saddened, and returned home to Salzburg.

By the time Wolfgang got there, Mr. Mozart had talked the archbishop into giving Wolfgang a job as court organist. The new job didn't last very long, though. Wolfgang and the archbishop still had big problems getting along. After a huge argument, the archbishop had Wolfgang kicked out of his palace!

Wolfgang's home in Salzburg

In 1781, Wolfgang Mozart left Salzburg for good. He decided to go to Vienna, a city where he had lots of friends. Even though the emperor's musicians had given him some problems a few years earlier, Wolfgang knew that Joseph II really appreciated his music.

It was in Vienna that Wolfgang fell in love with and married a singer named Constanze Weber. Wolfgang had some of the happiest times of his life in Vienna and wrote many of his greatest works there. But as time went on, Wolfgang got himself into money problems again.

Wolfgang's wife, Constanze Mozart

Wolfgang performing music for
Austrian emperor Joseph II

He often had to work day and night to
put on concerts and write music for special
occasions. Even with Constanze's help and
encouragement, Wolfgang Mozart's health
started getting worse and worse.

Some people feel that Wolfgang Mozart's most important musical achievement was his operas. After he moved to Vienna, Wolfgang wrote some of his greatest operas, like *The Marriage of Figaro*, *Don Giovanni*, and *The Magic Flute*.

During this time, there were two main types of operas. Serious ones, with stories about kings, gods, and heroes, were called *opera seria*. Funny ones about everyday people were called *opera buffa*. Wolfgang did an amazing thing by sometimes mixing these different styles in the same opera! He made his operas more interesting by showing that—as in real life—things aren't always just serious or just funny.

A set design for a scene from Mozart's opera *The Magic Flute*

In one of his most popular operas, *The Magic Flute*, Mozart combined all kinds of musical moods. There is the frightening, powerful music he wrote for the wise sorcerer, Sarastro, who sings some of the lowest and most serious notes ever. In another piece, the evil Queen of the Night sings some of the highest and fastest notes you'll ever hear!

Then there are the love songs that Prince Tamino and Princess Pamina sing to each other. Finally, there is the playful music written for the comedy characters Papageno the bird catcher and his girlfriend Papagena.

In one part, Mozart has them sing their names back and forth so quickly that they sound almost like an unusual instrument, especially the "Pa-Pa-Pa-Pa-Pa . . ." part. It's so much fun to listen to, you might find yourself trying to sing along to see if you can keep up with Papageno and Papagena.

Papageno, a character from *The Magic Flute*

A scene from Mozart's opera *Don Giovanni*

One of the greatest things Wolfgang Mozart was able to do in his operas was create music that gives you such a clear understanding of each character that you feel you almost know them, or know a lot about them.

Mozart composing the *Requiem* from his deathbed

After he finished *The Magic Flute*, Wolfgang Amadeus Mozart wasn't well at all. He used all the energy he had to compose a piece called *Requiem*, but died before he could finish it. Wolfgang was only 35 years old.

Wolfgang Amadeus Mozart wrote more than 800 pieces of music. It's usually hard for people to choose a favorite one, because so many of them are wonderful to listen to.

Almost all of Mozart's music seems to have a mysterious power and beauty to it. It's easy to hear Mozart's great music. You can go online and stream his music for free.

LEARN MORE BY TAKING THE MOZART QUIZ!

(ANSWERS ON THE NEXT PAGE.)

1. Both Wolfgang and his sister were child prodigies. What is a prodigy?
- **a** Someone who gently prods cattle with a stick to keep them from blocking the road.
- **b** A person who treats foot disorders.
- **c** A child who has super-remarkable talents and skills.

2. **TRUE or FALSE:** Mozart once bought a pet bird because it whistled a beautiful tune for him.

3. Mozart loved riddles and word games. He would often have fun with his name by scrambling letters around when he signed documents and letters. What were some of his favorite name scrambles?
- **a** Romatz
- **b** Trazom
- **c** Oz Mart
- **d** WAM

4. **TRUE or FALSE:** Even microbes (yes, microbes) enjoy Mozart's music.

5. Even though Mozart was popular and famous, he never seemed to have enough money. Why did such a great composer have money problems?
- **a** He wasted tons of money buying the latest fashionable clothes.
- **b** He insisted on living in a large expensive apartment and filling it with high-priced furniture and accessories.
- **c** Fewer people were paying to attend Mozart's concerts because they thought his music was becoming old-fashioned.
- **d** He spent way too much money on party-going and entertainment.
- **e** All of the above.

ANSWERS

1. **c** Prodigies are young children who have extraordinary talent. They usually have more knowledge than adults have in subjects such as music, math, or science. Wolfgang Amadeus Mozart is considered to have been a super-prodigy!

2. **TRUE** Mozart bought a pet starling when it whistled a beautiful song for him. The bird's song helped inspire Mozart's Piano Concerto No.17 in G Major!

3. **a and b** Mozart sometimes signed his name Romatz or Trazom on letters and business agreements. When he was in Italy, he had fun changing his first name to Wolfgango so it would sound more Italian.

4. **TRUE** A German sewage plant has played Mozart's music to make tiny waste-eating microbes work more efficently. Their favorite recording seems to be Mozart's opera *The Magic Flute*. Mozart's music also gets credit for helping cows produce more milk and increasing the intelligence of unborn babies.

5. **e** All of the above! Mozart was never very good at managing money. He enjoyed living well and overspent on just about everything. He often had to borrow from friends to pay his bills.

DEC. 2017

DEC 2017